LITTLE BOOK

⬦ OF ⬦

FROGS

WEIDENFELD & NICOLSON

LONDON

LA PRINCESSE ET LE ROI
DES GRENOUILLES
E. Payer c.1910

FROGS

MAIDEN'S KISS

I am a frog
I live under a spell
I live at the bottom
Of a green well

And here I must wait
Until a maiden places me
On her royal pillow
And kisses me
In her father's palace.

THE FROG PRINCE
Stevie Smith 1902–1971

A FROG HE WOULD
A-WOOING GO

A frog he would a-wooing go,
  Heigh ho! says Rowley,
A frog he would a-wooing go,
Whether his mother would let him or no
  With a rowley, powley, gammon and spinach,
  Heigh ho! says Anthony Rowley.

   So off he set with his opera hat,
    Heigh ho! says Rowley,
  And on the road he met a rat
    With a rowley, powley, gammon and spinach,
    Heigh ho! says Anthony Rowley.

'Pray, Mr Rat, will you go with me,
  Heigh ho! says Rowley,
Kind Mrs Mousey for to see?'
  With a rowley, powley, gammon and spinach,
  Heigh ho! says Anthony Rowley.

A FROG HE WOULD A-WOOING GO
Thomas Ravenscroft 1592–1640

A FROGGY A-WOOING

Bernhard Ollendorff

FROGS

Frogs and Snails

I marvel why frogs and snails are with some people, and in some countries, in great account, and judged wholesome food, where as indeed they have in them nothing else but a cold, gross, slimy and excremental juice.

VIA RECTA 1620
Tobias Venner

GOLDEN BELL FROG

Ferdinand Bauer 1760–1826

FROGS AND WATERLILIES
La Torre 1907

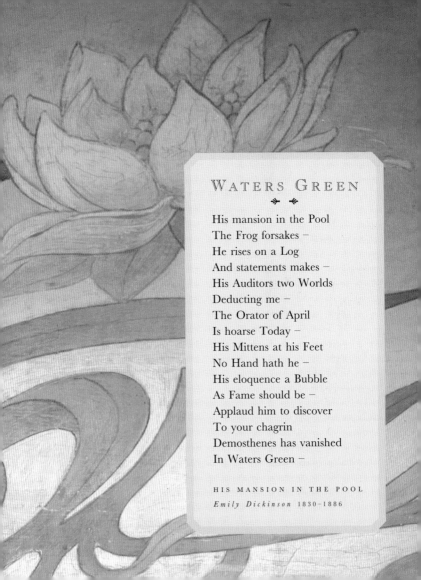

WATERS GREEN

➤ ◆ ◆

His mansion in the Pool
The Frog forsakes –
He rises on a Log
And statements makes –
His Auditors two Worlds
Deducting me –
The Orator of April
Is hoarse Today –
His Mittens at his Feet
No Hand hath he –
His eloquence a Bubble
As Fame should be –
Applaud him to discover
To your chagrin
Demosthenes has vanished
In Waters Green –

HIS MANSION IN THE POOL
Emily Dickinson 1830–1886

MR JEREMY FISHER READING

HIS NEWSPAPER

Beatrix Potter

FROGS

Once Upon a Time

——— ᠅ ———

Once upon a time there was a frog called Mr Jeremy Fisher; he lived in a little damp house amongst the buttercups at the edge of a pond.

The water was all slippy-sloppy in the larder and in the back passage.

But Mr Jeremy liked getting his feet wet; nobody ever scolded him, and he never caught cold!

from THE TALE OF MR JEREMY FISHER
Beatrix Potter 1866–1943

The Frog and the Toad

Hopping frog, hop here and be seen,
I'll not pelt you with stick or stone:
Your cap is laced and your coat is green;
Goodbye, we'll let each other alone.

Plodding toad, plod here and be looked at,
You the finger of scorn is crooked at:
But though you are lumpish, you're harmless too;
You won't hurt me, and I won't hurt you.

THE FROG AND THE TOAD
Christina Rossetti 1830–1894

PAN IN THE REEDS

Arnold Böcklin 1827–1901

GRATEFUL COOLNESS

I need not remind a gentleman of your extensive reading of the excellent account there is from Mr Derham, in Ray's Wisdom of God in the Creation concerning the migration of frogs from their breeding ponds. In this account he at once subverts that foolish opinion of their dropping from the clouds in rain; showing that it is from the grateful coolness and moisture of those showers that they are tempted to set out on their travels, which they defer till those fall.

from THE NATURAL HISTORY
OF SELBORNE
Gilbert White 1720–1793

LEAPFROG

FROGS

A Frog's Fate

Contemptuous of his home beyond
  The village and the village pond,
  A large-souled Frog who spurned each byeway
  Hopped along the imperial highway.

Nor grunting pig nor barking dog
  Could disconcert so great a Frog.
  The morning dew was lingering yet,
  His sides so cool, his tongue so wet:
  The night-dew, when the night should come,
  A travelled Frog would send him home.

Not so, alas! The wayside grass
  Sees him no more: not so, alas!
  A broad-wheeled waggon unawares
  Ran him down, his joys, his cares,
  From dying choke one feeble croak
  The Frog's perpetual silence broke: –
  'Ye buoyant Frogs, ye great and small,
  Even I am mortal after all!
  My road to fame turns out a wry way;
  I perish on the hideous highway;
  Oh for my familiar byeway!'

The croaking Frog sobbed and was gone;
The Waggoner strode whistling on,
Unconscious of the carnage done,
Whistling that Waggoner strode on –
Whistling (it may have happened so)
'A froggy would a-wooing go.'
A hypothetic frog trolled he,
Obtuse to reality.

from A FROG'S FATE
Christina Rossetti 1830–1894

THE EDIBLE FROG

FROG CARICATURE
Th. Heine 1901

FROGS

A Frog's Advantage

Most toads can swim if they're forced to, but unlike frogs, they rarely enter the water. Since the planet is two-thirds water, where do you think the limitations lie: with the frogs or the toads? Frogs are smooth and sleek and moist; toads are rough and dry and warty.

from HALF ASLEEP IN FROG PAJAMAS
Tom Robbins

FROGS

A STARTLED FROG

I love at early morn from new mown swath
To see the startled frog his rout pursue
And mark while leaping oer the dripping path
    His bright sides scatter dew
An early lark that from its bustle flyes –
    To hail his mattin new
    And watch him to the skyes.

from SUMMER IMAGES
John Clare 1793–1864

CHINESE WATERCOLOUR

21

The Frogs learn to jump
from the Fairies.

FROGGIE

By a quiet little stream on an old mossy log,
Looking very forlorn, sat a little green frog;
He'd a sleek speckled back, and two bright yellow eyes,
And when dining, selected the choicest of flies.

The sun was so hot he scarce opened his eyes,
Far too lazy to stir, let alone watch for flies,
He was nodding, and nodding, and almost asleep,
When a voice in the branches chirped: 'Froggie, cheep cheep!'

'You'd better take care,' piped the bird to the frog,
'In the water you'll be if you fall off that log.
Can't you see that the streamlet is up to the brim?'
Croaked the froggie: 'What odds! You forget I can swim!'

Then the froggie looked up at the bird perched so high
On a bough that to him seemed to reach to the sky;
So he croaked to the bird: 'If you fall, you will die!'
Chirped the birdie: 'What odds! You forget I can fly!'

THE FROG AND THE BIRD
Vera Hessey

FROGS

EDUCATED FROG

SMILEY...ketched a frog one day, and took him home, and he said he cal'lated to educate him; so he never done nothing for three months but set in his back yard and learn that frog to jump...He got him up so in the matter of ketching flies, and kep' him in practice so constant, that he'd nail a fly every time as fur as he could see him. Smiley said all a frog wanted was education, and he could do 'most anything – and I believe him. Why, I've seen him set Dan'l Webster – Dan'l Webster was the name of the frog – and sing out 'Flies, Dan'l, flies!' and quicker'n you could wink he'd spring straight up and snake a fly off'n the counter there, an flop down on the floor ag'n as solid as a glob of mud, and fall to scratching the side of his head with his hind foot as indifferent as if he hadn't no idea he been doin' any more'n any frog might do. You never see a frog so modest and straightfor'ard as he was, for all he was so gifted.

from THE CELEBRATED JUMPING FROG
OF CALAVERAS COUNTY
Mark Twain 1835–1910

24

FROGS

CONTENTMENT

from When All Is Young 1880s

FROGS

AGILE FROGS

from The Royal Natural History 1896

FROGS

Angler's Tip

Put your hook into his mouth, which you may easily do from the middle of April till August; and then the frog's mouth grows up and he continues so for at least six months without eating, but is sustained, none but He whose name is Wonderful knows how: I say, put your hook, I mean the arming-wire, through his mouth and out at his gills; and then with a fine needle and silk sew the upper part of his leg, with only one stitch, to the arming-wire of your hook; or tie the frog's leg, above the upper joint, to the armed-wire; and, in so doing, use him as though you loved him, that is, harm him as little as you may possibly, that he may live the longer.

from THE COMPLEAT ANGLER
Izaak Walton 1593–1683

The Frog

The Frog by Nature is both damp and cold,
Her Mouth is large, her belly much will hold:
She sits somewhat ascending, love to be
Croaking in Gardens, though unpleasantly.

THE FROG
John Bunyan 1628–1688

WARY PLAYMATES
Anonymous

FROGS

LÉZARDS ET GRENOUILLES

Bénédictus c.1900

Orchestral Frogs

Can these, indeed, be voices, that so greet
   The twilight still? I seem to hear
Oboe and cymbal in the rhythmic beat
   With bass-drum and bassoon; their drear
   And droll crescendo louder growing,
   Then falling back, like waters ebbing, flowing, –
Back to the silent sweet!

THE FROGS

Florence Earle Coates 1850–1927

A - h u m

A frog went a walking on a summer's day,
  A-hum, a-hum.
A frog went a walking on a summer's day,
He met Miss Mousie on the way,
  A-hum, a-hum, a-hum, a-hum, a-hum.

He said, 'Miss Mousie, will you marry me?'
  A-hum, a-hum.
He said, 'Miss Mousie, will you marry me?
We'll live together in an apple tree.'
  A-hum, a-hum, a-hum, a-hum, a-hum.

TRADITIONAL SONG

FROGS

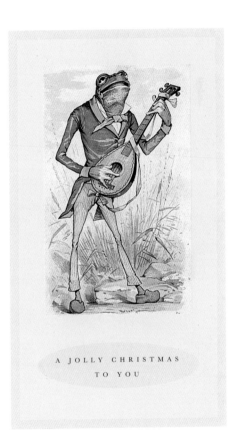

A JOLLY CHRISTMAS
TO YOU

FROGS

FROG AND TOAD

Croakle and Quackle

*S*peckled-black Toad and freckle-green Frog,
Hopping together from quay to bog;
From pool into puddle
Right on they huddle;
Through thick and through thin,
Without tail or fin;
Croakle goes first and *Quackle* goes after,
Plash in the flood
And plump in the mud,
With slippery heels
Vaulting over the eels,
And mouths to their middles split down
    into laughter
      Hu! hu! hex!

George Darley 1795–1846

FROGS

FROG CHORUS

'What a delightful voice you have!' cried the Frog. 'Really it is quite like a croak, and croaking is of course the most musical sound in the world. You will hear our glee-club this evening. We sit in the old duck-pond close by the farmer's house, and as soon as the moon rises we begin. It is so entrancing that everybody lies awake to listen to us. In fact, it was only yesterday that I heard the farmer's wife say to her mother that she could not get a wink of sleep at night on account of us. It is most gratifying to find oneself so popular.'

THE REMARKABLE ROCKET
Oscar Wilde 1854–1900

FROGS

FRENCH CROAKING FROGS

from The Wind in the Willows
Arthur Rackham

FROGS

Justly Sensitive

*B*e kind and tender to the Frog,
  And do not call him names,
As 'Slimy skin', or 'Polly-wog',
  Or likewise 'Ugly James'.

      *O*r 'Gape-a-grin', or 'Toad-gone-wrong',
        Or 'Billy Bandy-knees';
      The Frog is justly sensitive
        To epithets as these.

            *N*o animal will more repay
              A treatment kind and fair;
            At least so lonely people say
            Who keep a Frog (and, by the way,
              They are extremely rare).

THE FROG

Hilaire Belloc 1870–1953

FROGS AND DUCK

ong pull, and a pull all together

A DELICACY

I have been in France,
  and have eaten frogs.
The nicest little rabbity
  things you ever tasted.

Charles Lamb
1774–1834

FROGS

FROGS

JUST SITTING AROUND

The frogs all sit around in threes and fours
Like fat politicians discussing laws.
But if you want some action just walk by
There will be lots of plopping as they fly
Into their little pond, all safe and sound,
Waiting to return for another round
Of sitting around, just sitting around
Till a fly disappears without a sound.

JUST SITTING AROUND

Isaac Stewart

GRANDFATHER FROG

Fat green frog sits by the pond,
Big frog, bull frog, grandfather frog.
Croak–croak–croak.
Shuts his eye, opens his eye,
Rolls his eye, winks his eye,
Waiting for
A little fat fly.

Croak, croak.
I go walking down by the pond,
I want to see the big green frog,
I want to stare right into his eye,
Rolling, winking, funny old eye.
But oh! he heard me coming by.
Croak–croak–
SPLASH!

GRANDFATHER FROG
Louise Seaman Bechtel

FROGS

HORNED FROG

*from The Royal Natural
History* 1896

FROGS HOPPING OVER ROCKS

Sobum

FROG WISDOM

There are not frogs wherever there is water; but wherever there are frogs, water will be found.

SPRÜCHE IN PROSA
Johann von Goethe 1749–1832

FROGS

The Brown Frog

*T*o-day as I went out to play
I saw a brown frog in the way,
I know that frogs are smooth and green,
But this was brown – what could it mean?
I asked a lady in the road;
She said it was a spotted toad!

THE BROWN FROG
Mary K. Robinson

FROGS

CRAPAUDS
after Oudart 19th century

VIRGIN ENTHRONED
WITH CHILD (detail)
Antonio da Negroponte

FROGS

A Wonderful Bird

What a wonderful bird the frog are.
When he sit he stand almost.
When he hop he fly almost.
He ain't got no sense hardly.
He ain't got no tail hardly neither
Where he sit almost.

Anonymous

FROGS

WIGGLE! WAGGLE!

*U*nderneath the water-weeds
　Small and black, I wriggle,
And life is most surprising!
　Wiggle! waggle! wiggle!

*T*here's every now and then a most
　Exciting change in me,
I wonder, wiggle! waggle!
　What I shall turn out to be!

THE TADPOLE
E. E. Gould

FROGS

THEIR FIRST LESSON
IN SWIMMING

DIVERS ESPÈCES DE
GRENOUILLES

Frogs, the Earth and the Stars

As you erudite people well know, the word *amphibian* comes from the Greek *amphi* and *bios*, meaning to live a double life. This refers, needless to say, to an ability to live both in water and on land. In that regard, amphibians are the most adaptable creatures in the world, the ones, ironically, best suited for residence here. But as those of you who've read spy stories or had extramarital affairs are aware, a double life implies a clandestine life, a life of secret behaviors. Now, a frog is a little dumb animal with a poot-sized brain. It probably isn't the custodian of a hell of a lot of covert information. No, indeed. But rather than possessing secrets, suppose a frog *is* a secret. A secret link…The amphibian is the bridge between the terrestrial and the aquatic. I invite you to consider that it may also be a bridge between our water planet and the largely arid galaxy. A bridge between earth and the stars.

from HALF ASLEEP IN FROG PAJAMAS
Tom Robbins

Acknowledgements

Designed and created by
THE BRIDGEWATER BOOK COMPANY
Words chosen by JOANNE JESSOP
Picture research by FELICITY COX *and*
VANESSA FLETCHER
Page make-up by JANE LANAWAY
Printed in Italy

*The publishers wish to thank the following for
the use of pictures:*
ARCHIV FUR KUNST AND GESCHICHTE,
London: p.50; Neue Pinakothek, Munich
p.13. J.L. CHARMET, Paris: back cover, p.2;
Bibliothèque des Arts Décoratifs pp.18, 30, 49,
54. CHRISTIES IMAGES: front cover. E.T.
ARCHIVE: front cover, title page, pp.8–9;
Victoria & Albert Museum pp.46–7. FINE ART
PHOTOGRAPHIC LIBRARY: pp.28–9 Reproduced
by permission of FREDERICK WARNE & CO.: p.10
(Copyright © Frederick Warne & Co., 1906,
1987), p.42 (Copyright © Frederick Warne
& Co., 1984, 1995). MARY EVANS PICTURE
LIBRARY: pp.17, 22, 25. NATURAL HISTORY
MUSEUM: p.7. RETROGRAPH ARCHIVE/MARTIN
BREEZE: pp.5, 14–15, 33, 34,37,40–1, 53.

*The publishers gratefully acknowledge permission
to reproduce the following material in this book:*

p.3 *The Frog Prince* by Stevie Smith from *The
Collected Poems of Stevie Smith* (Penguin 20th
Century Classics) by permission of James
MacGibbon. p.11 *The Tale of Jeremy Fisher* by
Beatrix Potter © F Warne & Co., 1906; by
permission of Frederick Warne & Co.
pp.19 and 55 Extracts from *Half Asleep in Frog
Pajamas* by Tom Robbins by permission of the
author and Bantam Books. p.39 *The Frog* by
Hilaire Belloc reprinted by permission of Peters
Fraser & Dunlop Group Ltd. p.43 *Just Sitting
Around* by Isaac Stewart by permission of the
author. p.44 *Grandfather Frog* by Louis Seaman
Bechtel taken from *Another Here and Now Story
Book* by permission of F. P. Dutton and Co.

*Every effort has been made
to trace all copyright holders
and obtain permissions.
The editor and publishers
sincerely apologise for
any inadvertent errors or
omissions and will be happy
to correct them in any future edition.*